Elvis Presley for Ukulele

Arranged by Jim Beloff

ISBN 978-1-4234-6556-0

HAL•LEONARD® CORPORATION

7777 W. BLUEMOUND RD. P.O. BOX 13819 MILWAUKEE, WI 53213

www.elvis.com

Visit Hal Leonard Online at
www.halleonard.com

My Hound Dog Has Fleas!

Although Elvis may have left the building, the songs he made famous are very much alive and well. They also translate really well to the ukulele. You'll find the arrangements here easy and fun to play. First, though, a few notes so that you can maximize your enjoyment.

1. Arrangements: Elvis had a remarkably wide vocal range with the ability to hit high notes ("Jailhouse Rock") and low notes ("Loving You"), sometimes both in the same song ("Heartbreak Hotel" and "Love Me"). In most cases we kept the arrangement in the original recorded key if it was a good ukulele key. For the G–C–E–A tuning (My Dog Has Fleas), the most player-friendly keys are C, F, G, and D. Where the original key was not uke-friendly we typically lowered it to an easier-to-play key.

2. Hawaiian D7: Most uke books diagram the D7 chord as seen here:

There is an alternative D7 that looks like this:

This version is sometimes known as the *Hawaiian D7* and often blends better with other uke chords. You'll find it featured in "Blue Hawaii."

3. First Note: You'll notice a grid at the start of every song that refers to the "First note." If you play the note where the dot or the open string is (identified with an "o") you'll hear the first singing note of the song:

First note

4. How to Use Tab: Two of the songs included here ("Heartbreak Hotel" and "I Need Your Love Tonight") feature uke solos. Based on the original guitar solos, these arrangements utilize uke tablature that tells you which strings are played at which frets. The four lines of the tab staff correspond to the four strings of the uke—first string (A) at the top—and the numbers written on the lines indicate which frets should be fingered. Numbers stacked on top of each other should be played together. The rhythmic values are shown using ovals, stems, and dots.

5. Suggested Strums: Most of the up-tempo rock 'n' roll songs here will be well-served with a solid down/up strum. Keep a look out for the N.C. symbol (no chord), though, in songs like "Blue Suede Shoes" where there are specific breaks in the strum. Another handy strum has a syncopated feel to it that works well with "It's Now or Never," "Loving You," and "Suspicious Minds." It is a combination of quick down/up strums plus a *roll*. In a typical four-beat measure it would look like this:

D   Roll U   U D   U
One and **Two** and **Three** and **Four** and**...**

I play the downstroke with the pad of my thumb and the upstroke with the pad of my index finger. The roll is made by running the ring, middle, and index fingers quickly in succession across the strings.

Enjoy!
Jim Beloff

All Shook Up

Words and Music by Otis Blackwell and Elvis Presley

First note

Moderately

1. Oh, well, — bless a, my soul, oh, what's _ wrong with me? I'm

itch - in' like a man _ on a fuz - zy tree. My friends say I'm act - in'

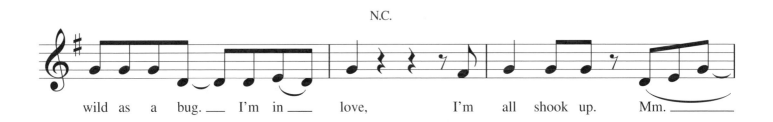

wild as a bug. _ I'm in _ love, I'm all shook up. Mm. _

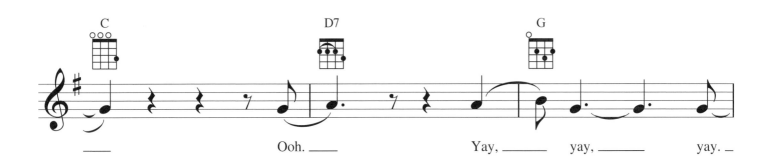

_ Ooh. _ Yay, _ yay, _ yay. _

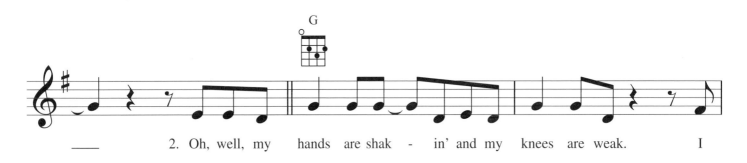

_ 2. Oh, well, my hands are shak - in' and my knees are weak. I

can't seem to stand __ on my own two feet. Who _____ do you thank __ when you

N.C.

have such luck? I'm in __ love, I'm all shook up. Mm. _____

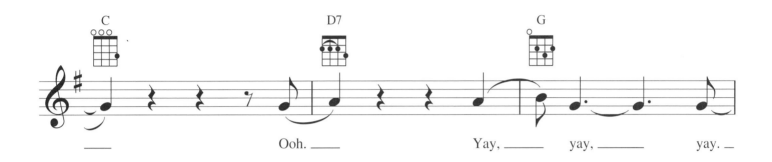

C   D7   G

_____ Ooh. __ Yay, _____ yay, _____ yay. __

C

_____ Well, a, please __ don't ask __ me what's a, on my mind. __ I'm a

G   C

lit - tle mixed up, __ but I feel fine. __ When I'm near the girl __ that

D7   N.C.

I love best, __ my heart beats so, it scares _____ me to death. 3. When she touched __

my hand, oh, what a chill I got. Her lips are like _ a vol -

ca - no that's hot. I'm ___ proud to say that she's my but - ter - cup. _ I'm in ___

love, I'm all shook up. Mm. ___ Ooh. _

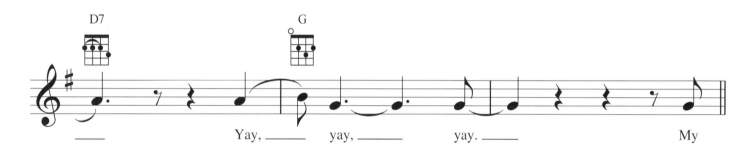

_ Yay, ___ yay, ___ yay. ___ My

tongue gets tied when I try to speak. My in - sides shake _ like a

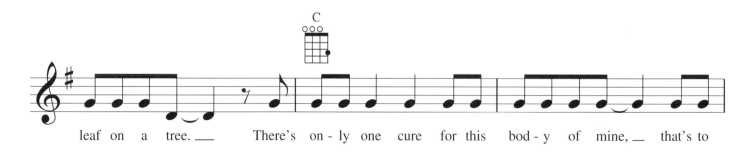

leaf on a tree. _ There's on - ly one cure for this bod - y of mine, _ that's to

have that girl and a love so fine. 4. When she touched __ my hand, __ oh, what a

chill I got. Her lips are like __ a vol - ca - no that's hot. I'm __

__ proud to say that she's my but - ter - cup. __ I'm in __ love, uh, I'm

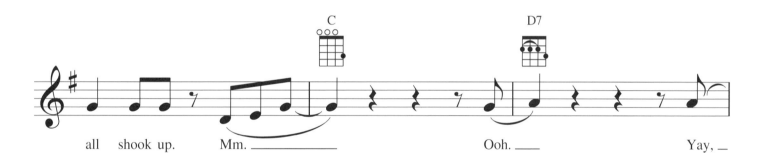

all shook up. Mm. ____ Ooh. ____ Yay, __

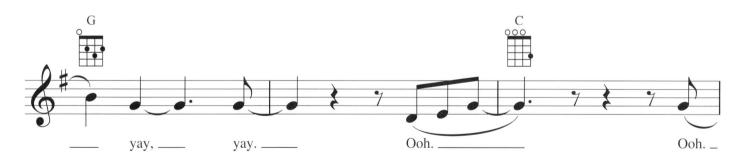

__ yay, __ yay. ____ Ooh. ____ Ooh. __

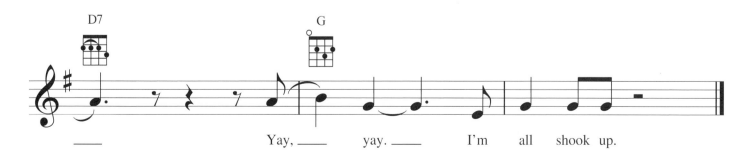

__ Yay, __ yay. ____ I'm all shook up.

Blue Hawaii

from the Paramount Picture WAIKIKI WEDDING
Words and Music by Leo Robin and Ralph Rainger

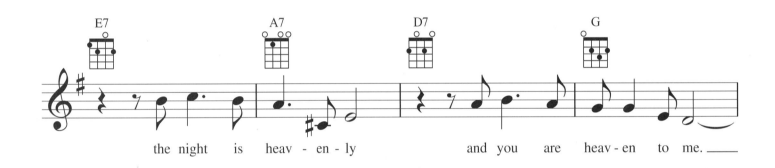

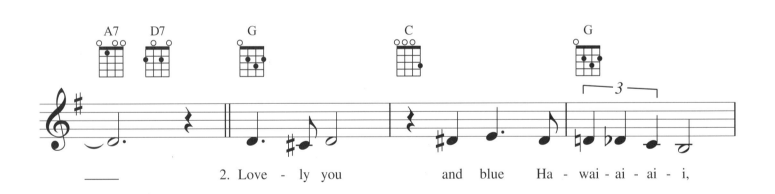

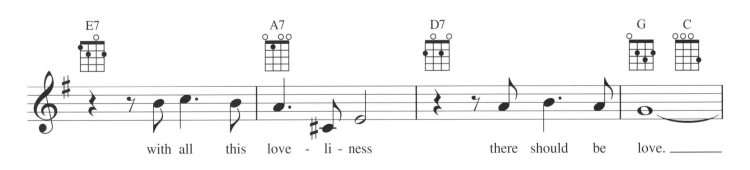

Come with me _____ while the moon is on the sea. _____ The night is young _____ and so _____ are we, so are we.

3., 4. Dreams come true in blue Ha - wai - ai - ai - i and mine could all come true this mag - ic

1. night of nights with you.

2. you.

Blue Suede Shoes

from G.I. BLUES

Words and Music by Carl Lee Perkins

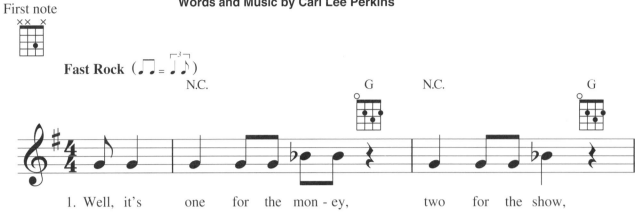

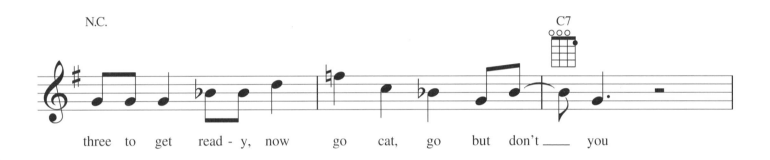

1. Well, it's one for the mon - ey, two for the show,

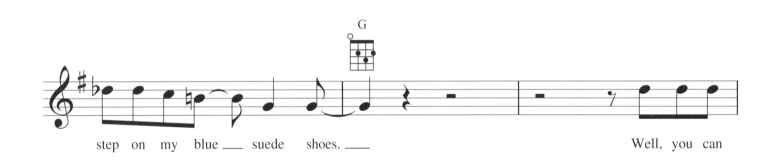

three to get read - y, now go cat, go but don't ____ you

step on my blue ____ suede shoes. ____ Well, you can

do an - y - thing, ____ but stay off of my blue ____ suede shoes.

2. Well, you can   knock   me   down, ___   step   on   my   face, ___
(3.) burn   my   house, ___   steal   my   car, ___

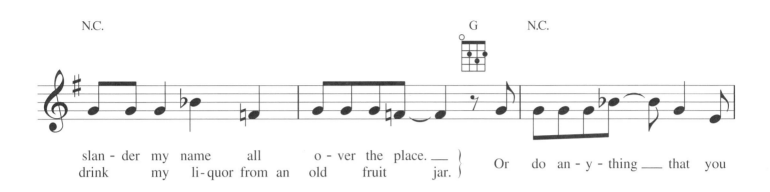

slan - der   my   name   all   o - ver   the   place. ___   Or   do   an - y - thing ___ that   you
drink   my   li - quor from an   old   fruit   jar.

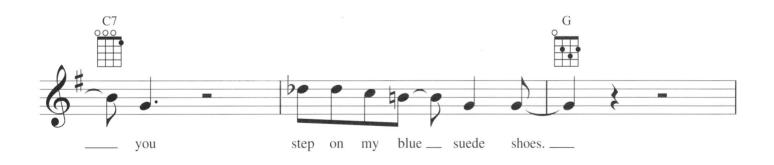

wan - na   do, ___   but   uh,   uh,   hon - ey,   lay   off ___ of   them   shoes.   And   don't ___

___ you   step   on   my   blue ___ suede   shoes. ___

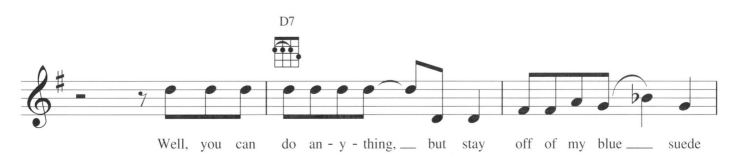

Well,   you   can   do   an - y - thing, ___ but   stay   off   of   my   blue ___ suede

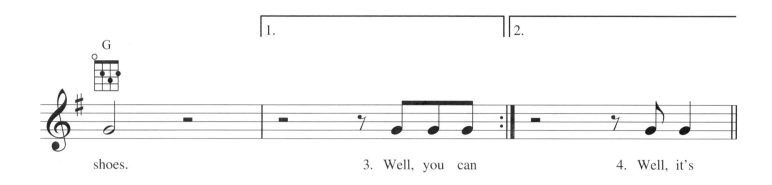

shoes.   3. Well, you can   4. Well, it's

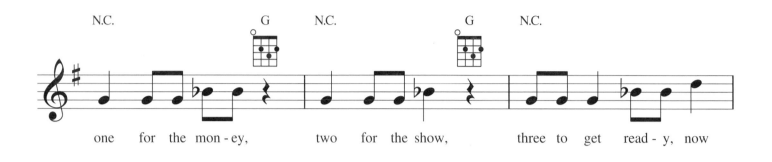

one   for the mon - ey,   two for the show,   three to get read - y, now

go,   go,   go, but don't ___ you   step on my blue __ suede shoes. __

___   Well, you can   do an - y - thing, __ but stay

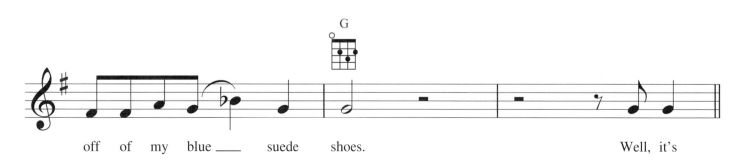

off of my blue ___ suede shoes.   Well, it's

blue,   blue,   blue suede shoes.   Blue,   blue,   blue __

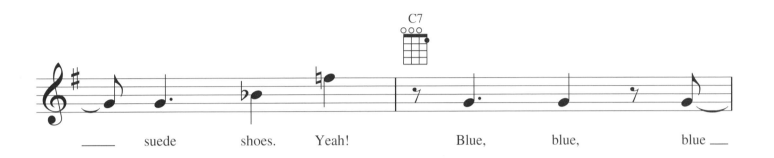

___ suede   shoes.   Yeah!   Blue,   blue,   blue ___

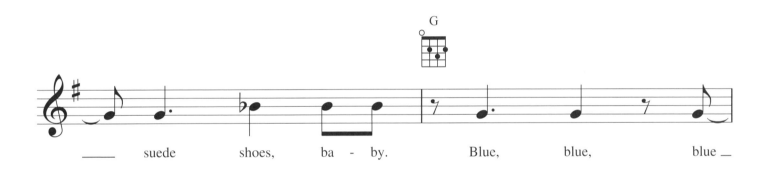

___ suede   shoes,   ba - by.   Blue,   blue,   blue __

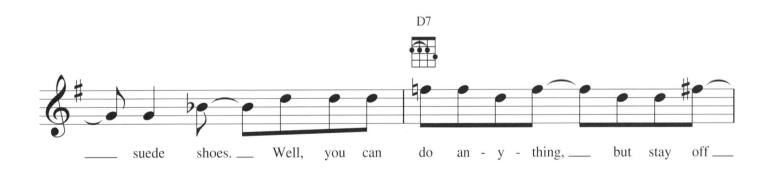

___ suede   shoes. __ Well, you can   do an - y - thing, ___ but stay off ___

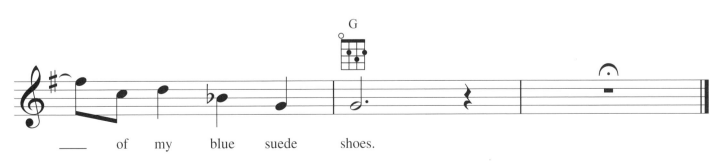

___ of   my   blue   suede   shoes.

Can't Help Falling in Love

from the Paramount Picture BLUE HAWAII
Words and Music by George David Weiss, Hugo Peretti and Luigi Creatore

you?   Like a ___ riv-er flows ___ sure-ly ___ to the sea,

dar-ling, ___ so it goes, ___ some things ___ are ___ meant to be.

3., 4. Take   my   hand,   take   my   whole   life

too,   for I can't   help ___ fall-ing ___ in ___

love ___ with   you.   you.   For I can't

help ___ fall-ing ___ in ___ love ___ with   you.

Crying in the Chapel

Words and Music by Artie Glenn

First note

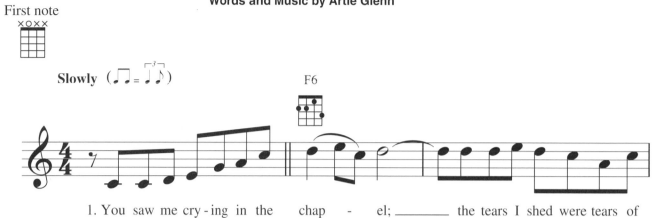

Slowly

1. You saw me cry-ing in the chap - el; _____ the tears I shed were tears of

joy. _____ I know the mean-ing of con - tent - ment, _____

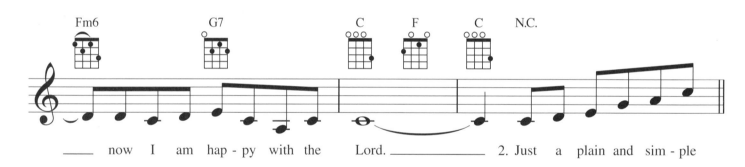

_____ now I am hap-py with the Lord. _____ 2. Just a plain and sim-ple

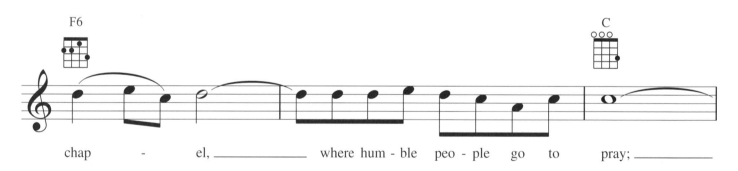

chap - el, _____ where hum-ble peo-ple go to pray; _____

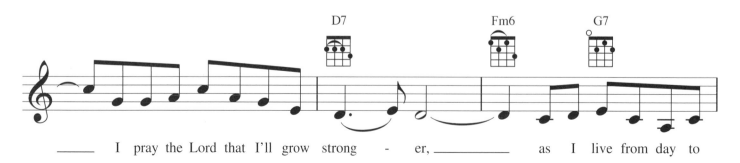

_____ I pray the Lord that I'll grow strong - er, _____ as I live from day to

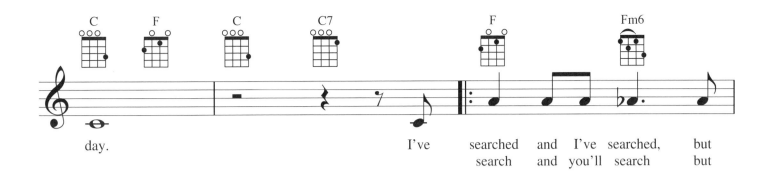

day.   I've   searched   and   I've searched,   but
                                  search   and   you'll   search   but

I   could-n't find   no   way on earth to gain peace of   mind. 3. Now I'm hap-py in the
you'll nev-er find   no   way on earth to gain peace of   mind. 4. Take your trou-bles to the

chap - el, _____   where peo - ple   are   of   one ac - cord; _____
chap - el, _____   get down   on   your knees and   pray; _____

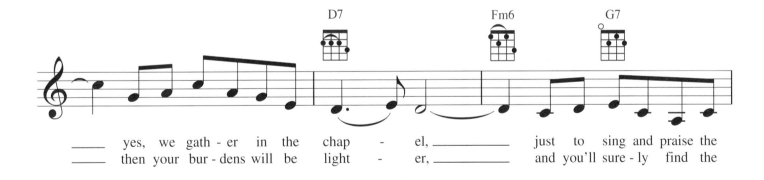

___ yes, we gath-er   in   the   chap - el, _____   just   to sing and praise the
___ then your bur-dens will be   light - er, _____   and you'll sure-ly find the

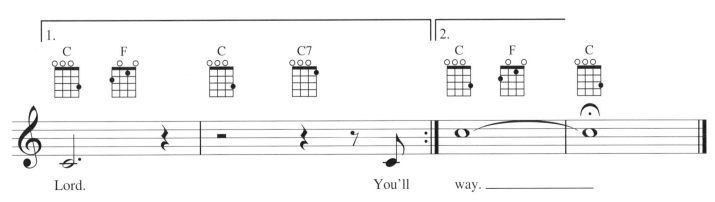

Lord.   You'll   way. _____

Don't

Words and Music by Jerry Leiber and Mike Stoller

First note

Moderately slow

1. "Don't, don't," that's what you say ___
2. Don't, don't leave my em - brace ___
3. don't, don't, don't feel that way. ___

___ each time that I hold ___ you this ___
___ for here in my arms ___ is your ___
___ I'm your love and yours ___ I will ___

way. When I feel like this and I want _ to
place. When the night grows cold and I want _ to
stay. This you can be - lieve, I will nev - er

kiss you, ba - by, don't say "don't."   "don't."
hold you, ba - by, don't say
leave you, Heav - en knows I

If   you   think   that   this   is   just   a

game   I'm   play - ing, _____   if   you   think   that

D.C. al Coda

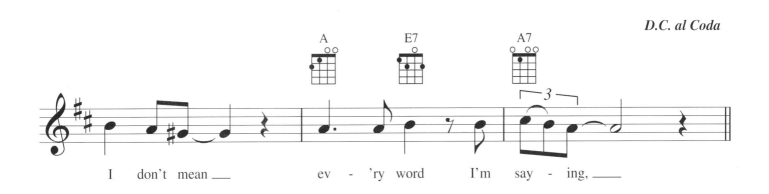

I   don't mean ___   ev - 'ry word   I'm   say - ing, ___

Coda

won't.   Ba - by, don't say "don't."

Don't Be Cruel
(To a Heart That's True)

Words and Music by Otis Blackwell and Elvis Presley

First note

Moderately fast

1. Well, you _ know I can be found sit - tin' home all a - lone.

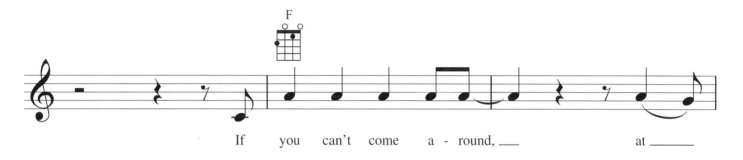

If you can't come a - round, ___ at _____

least, please, tel - e - phone. A don't be cruel

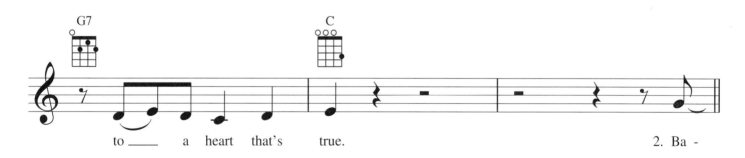

to ___ a heart that's true. 2. Ba -

- by, if I made you mad for some - thin' I might have said,

way.   Come   on   o - ver here and love   me.   You

know   what I want you to   say.   A don't be   cruel   to   a heart that's

true.   Why   should we   be   a - part?   I

real - ly   love you, ba   -   by, cross my   heart.   4. Well, let's _

walk up   to the preach - er   and let us say   "I   do."

Then you'll know you   have me,   and I'll   know that a I'll have   you.   A don't be

Heartbreak Hotel

Words and Music by Mae Boren Axton, Tommy Durden and Elvis Presley

First note

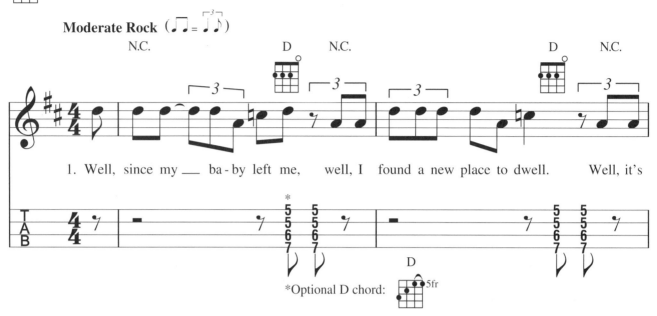

*Optional D chord:

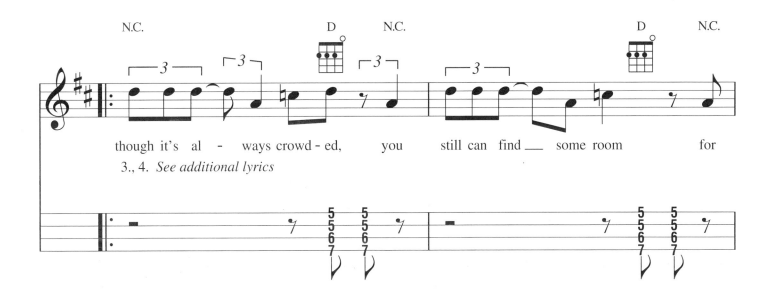

though it's al - ways crowd - ed, you still can find ___ some room for

3., 4. *See additional lyrics*

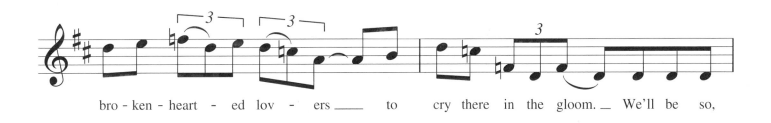

bro - ken - heart - ed lov - ers ___ to cry there in the gloom. ___ We'll be so,

we'll be so lone - ly, ba - by, we'll be so lone - ly.

Well, they're so lone - ly, ___ they could die. 3. Now, the die.

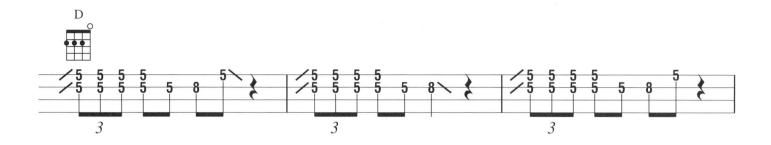

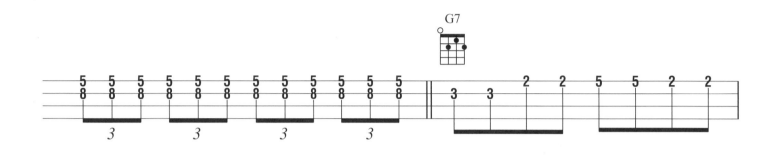

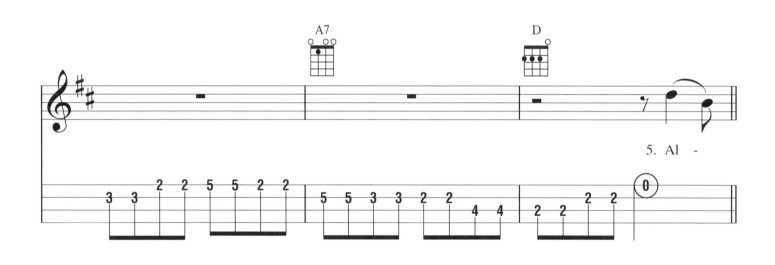

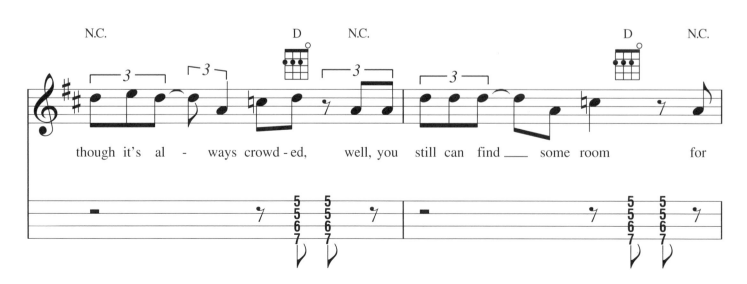

though it's al - ways crowd-ed, well, you still can find ___ some room   for

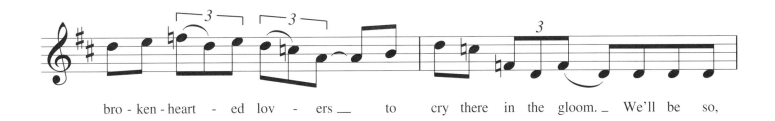

bro - ken - heart - ed lov - ers __ to cry there in the gloom. __ We'll be so,

we'll be so lone - ly, ba - by, well, they're so lone - ly, ___

we'll be so lone - ly ___ they could die. ___

Additional Lyrics

3. Now, the bellhop's tears keep flowin', the desk clerk's dressed in black,
   Well, they've been so long on Lonely Street they'll never, never gonna look back and they're so...
   They'll be so lonely, baby. Well, they're so lonely.
   Well, they're so lonely they could die.

4. Well, now if your baby leaves ya and you got a tale to tell,
   Well, just take a walk down Lonely Street to Heartbreak Hotel where you will be...
   You'll be so lonely, baby; where you will be lonely.
   You'll be so lonely you could die.

Hound Dog

Words and Music by Jerry Leiber and Mike Stoller

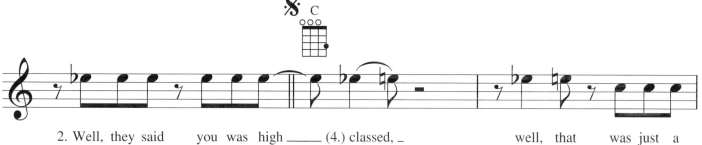

1. You ain't noth-in' but a hound dog, __ a, cry-in' all the time. You ain't __ noth-in' but a hound dog, __ a, cry-in' all the time. Well, __ you ain't nev-er caught a rab-bit and you ain't no friend of mine. __

2. Well, they said you was high __ (4.) classed, __ well, that was just a

lie.   Yeah, they said   you was high ___ classed, ___

well,   that   was just a   lie.   Yeah, ___ you ain't

To Coda ⊕

nev - er caught a rab - bit and you   ain't   no   friend   of   mine. _____

3. You ain't noth - in' but a   hound dog, ___ a,   cry - in' all the

time.   You ain't a, noth - in' but a   hound   dog, ___ a,

cry - in' all the   time.   Well, ___ you ain't

nev - er caught a rab - bit and you ain't no friend of mine. _____

D.S. al Coda

⊕ **Coda**

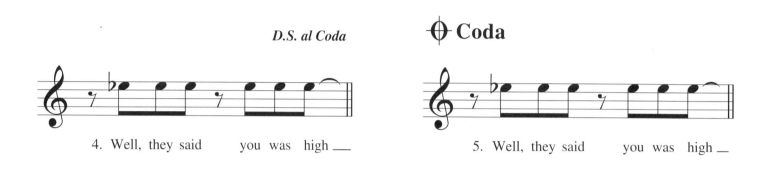

4. Well, they said   you was high __

5. Well, they said   you was high __

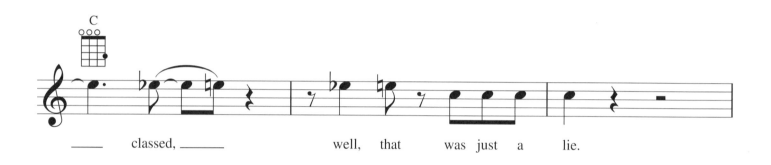

___ classed, _____   well, that was just a lie.

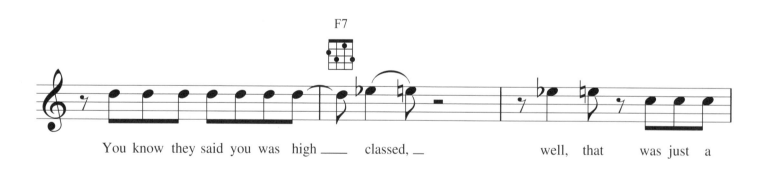

You know they said you was high ___ classed, ___   well, that was just a

lie.   Well, ___ you ain't   nev - er caught a rab - bit and you

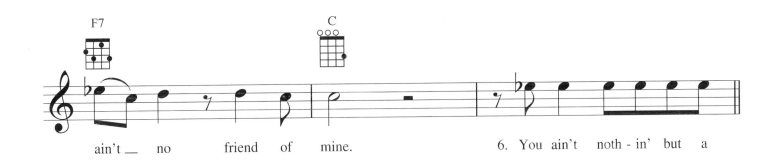

ain't — no friend of mine. 6. You ain't noth - in' but a

hound dog, — a, cry - in' all the time.

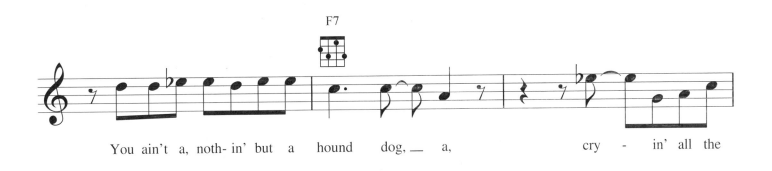

You ain't a, noth- in' but a hound dog, — a, cry - in' all the

time. Well, — you ain't nev - er caught a rab - bit, you

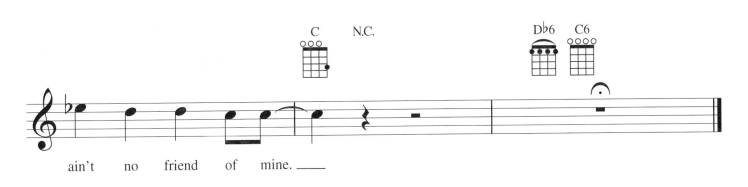

ain't no friend of mine. ——

It's Now or Never

Words and Music by Aaron Schroeder and Wally Gold

First note

Moderate Latin beat

It's now or nev - er; _____ come hold me

tight.   Kiss me, my dar - lin', _____

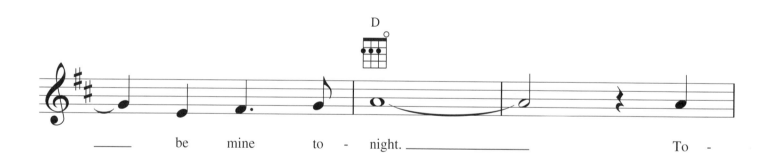

_____ be mine to - night. _____   To -

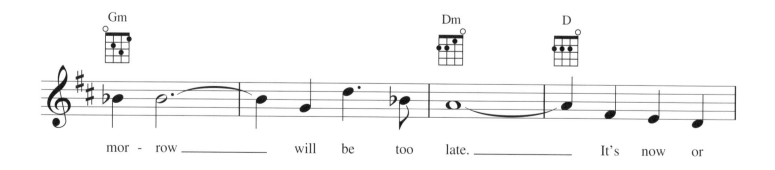

mor - row _____ will be too late. _____ It's now or

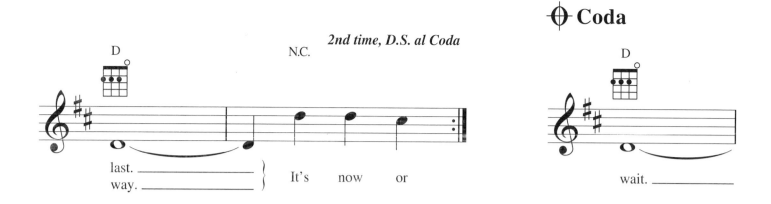

⊕ Coda

2nd time, D.S. al Coda

last. _____
way. _____ } It's now or

wait. _____

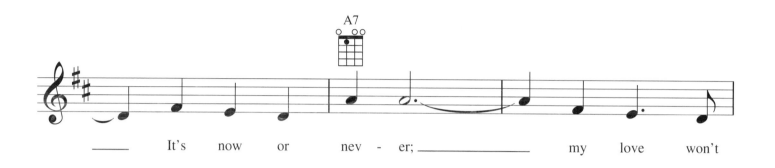

_____ It's now or nev - er; _____ my love won't

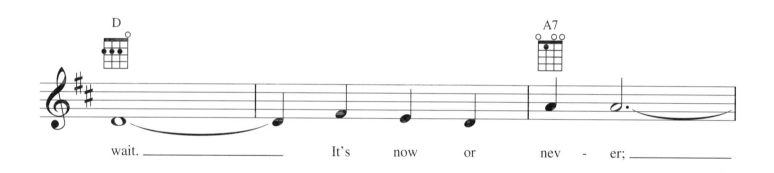

wait. _____ It's now or nev - er; _____

_____ my love won't wait. _____ It's now or

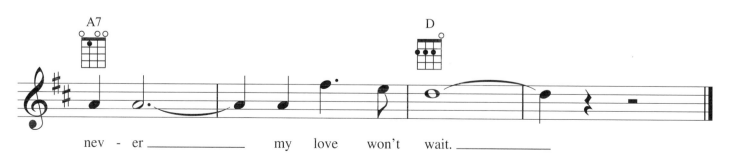

nev - er _____ my love won't wait. _____

I Need Your Love Tonight

Words and Music by Sid Wayne and Bix Reichner

First note

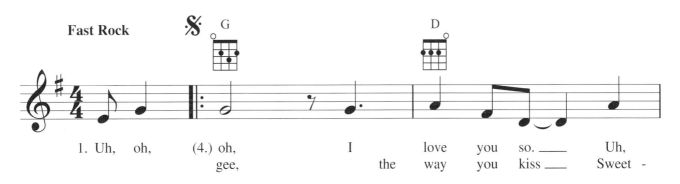

1. Uh, oh, (4.) oh, I love you so. ___ Uh,
gee, the way you kiss ___ Sweet -

uh, I can't let you go. ___ Ooh, ooh, don't
ie, too good to miss. ___ Wow - ie, I want

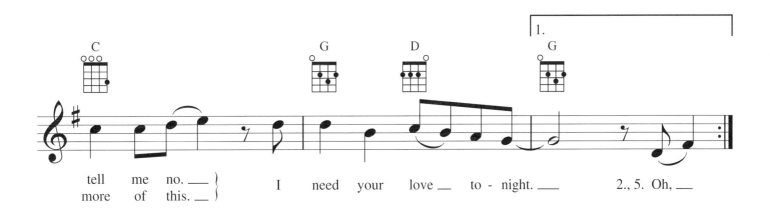

tell me no. ___ }
more of this. ___ }

I need your love ___ to - night. ___ 2., 5. Oh, ___

___ I've been wait - ing just for to - night ___ to

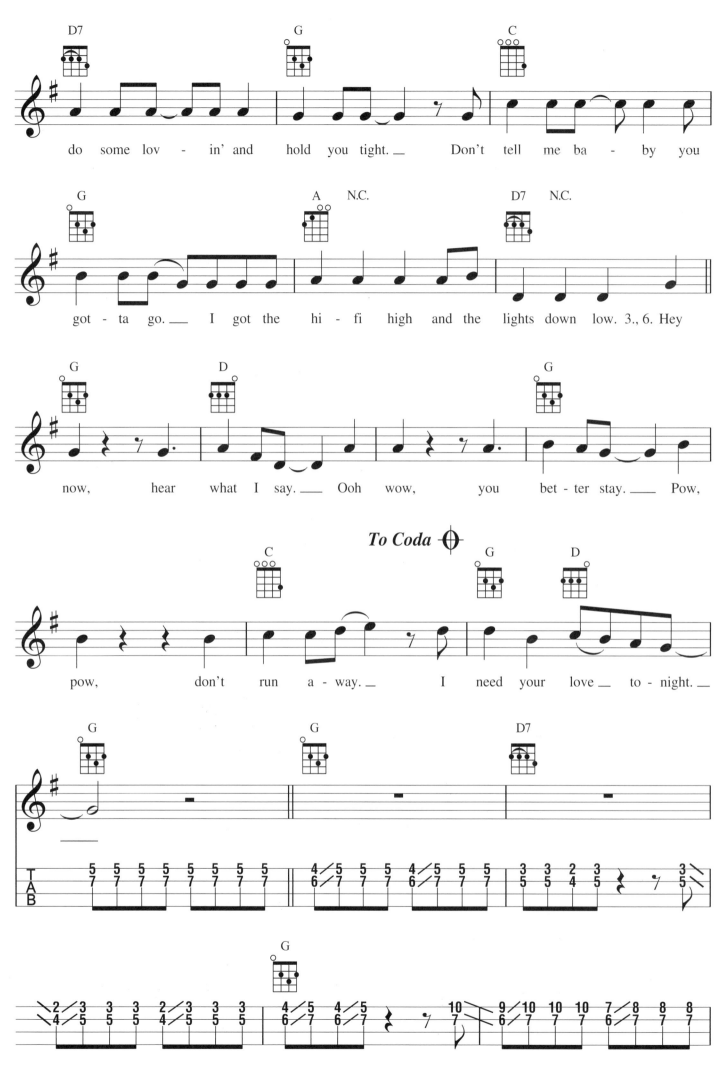

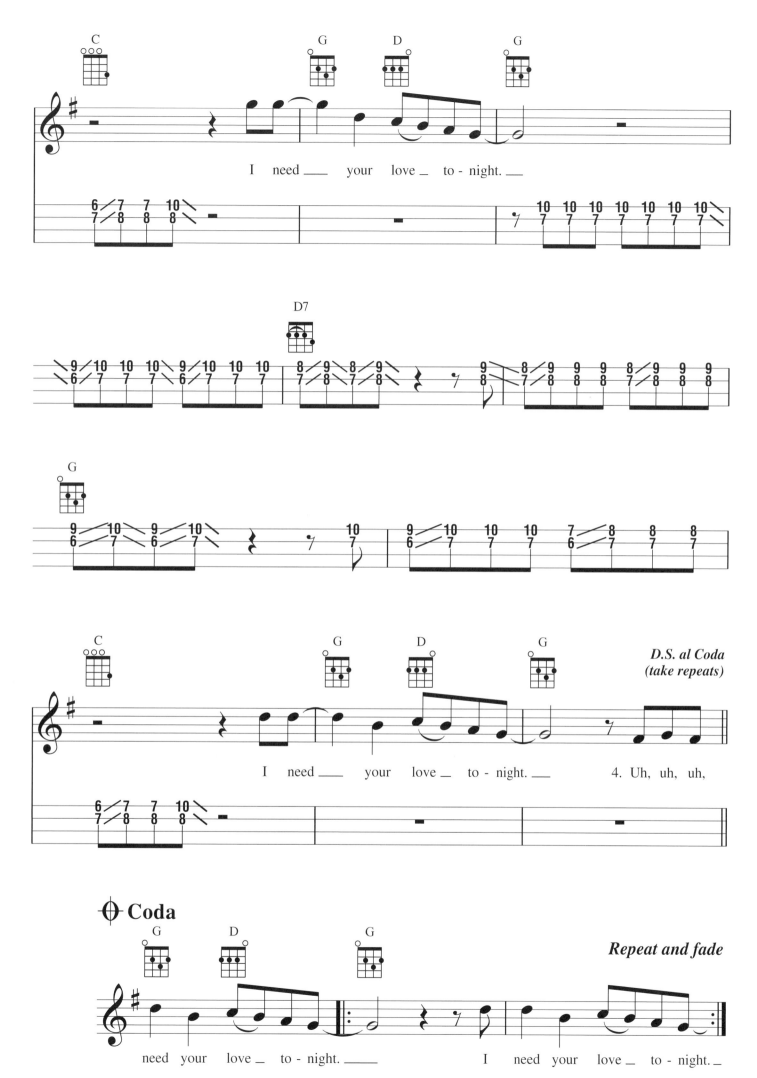

I Want You, I Need You, I Love You

Words and Music by Maurice Mysels and Ira Kosloff

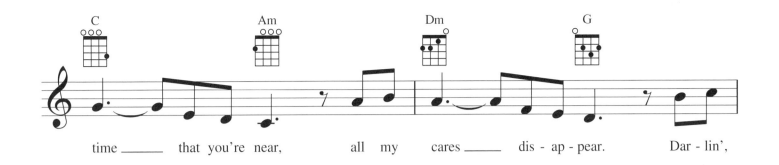

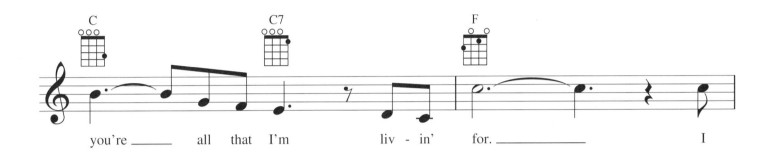

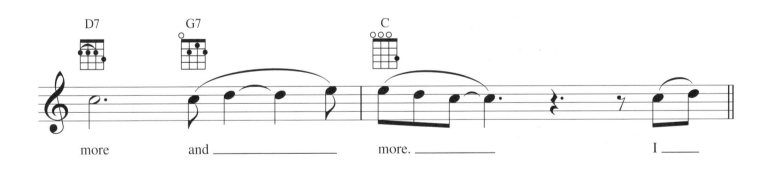

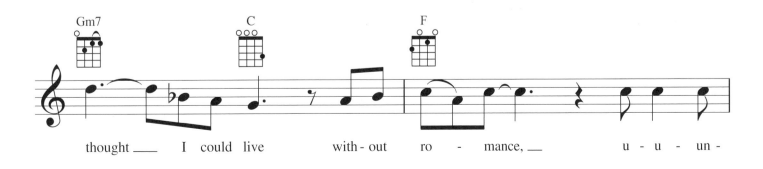

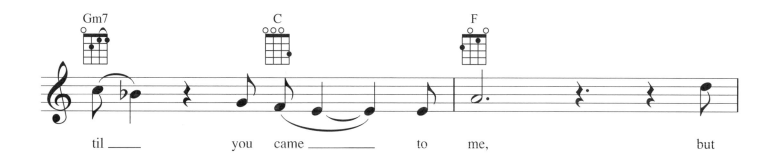

til _____ you came _____ to me, but

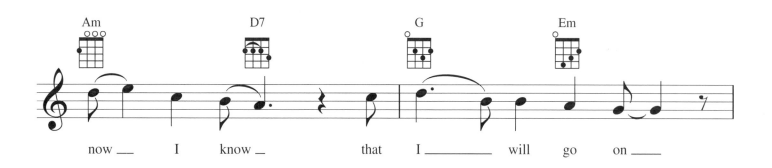

now __ I know __ that I _____ will go on _____

lov - ing you ___ e - ter - nal - ly. 3. Won't _____ you

(4.) please _____ be my own? __ Nev - er leave ____ me a - lone, 'cause I

die _____ ev - 'ry time we're a - part. I

Jailhouse Rock

Words and Music by Jerry Leiber and Mike Stoller

First note

Fast Rock

1. War - den threw a par - ty in the coun - ty jail. ___ The
2.-5. *See additional lyrics*

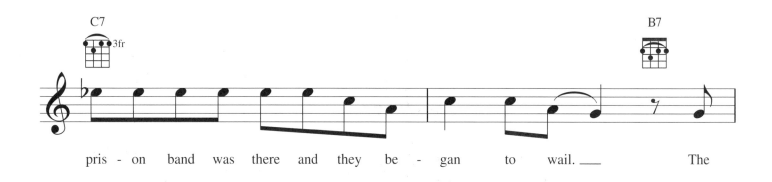

pris - on band was there and they be - gan to wail. ___ The

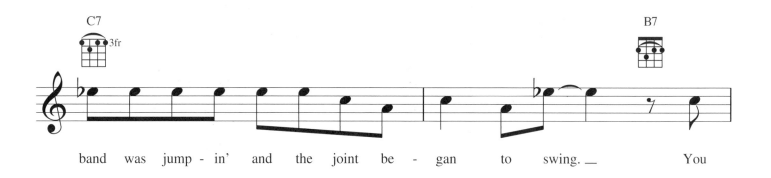

band was jump - in' and the joint be - gan to swing. ___ You

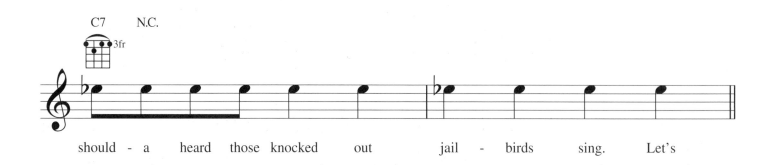

should - a heard those knocked out jail - birds sing. Let's

Additional Lyrics

2. Spider Murphy played the tenor saxophone
   Little Joe was blowin' on the slide trombone.
   The drummer boy from Illinois went crash, boom, bang!
   The whole rhythm section was the Purple Gang.

3. Number Forty-Seven said to Number Three,
   "You're the cutest jailbird I ever did see,
   I sure would be delighted with your company,
   Come on and do the Jailhouse Rock with me."

4. Sad sack was sittin' on a block of stone,
   Way over in the corner weeping all alone.
   The warden said, "Hey, buddy, don't you be no square,
   If you can't find a partner, use a wooden chair!"

5. Shifty Henry said to Bugs, "For heaven's sake,
   No one's lookin', now's our chance to make a break."
   Bugsy turned to Shifty and he said: "Nix, nix;
   I wanna stick around a while and get my kicks."

Love Me

Words and Music by Jerry Leiber and Mike Stoller

First note

1. Treat me like a fool, ___ treat me mean and cruel, ___ but ___

love me. Break ___ my faith-ful heart, tear it all a-

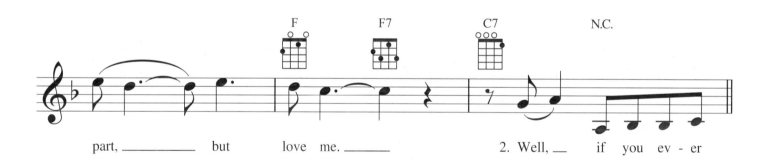

part, ___ but love me. ___ 2. Well, ___ if you ev-er

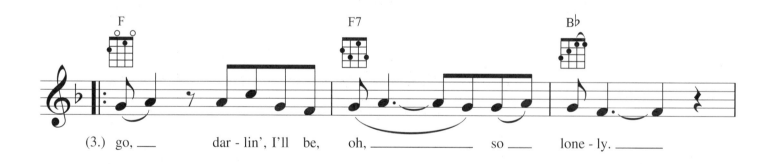

(3.) go, ___ dar-lin', I'll be, oh, ___ so ___ lone-ly.

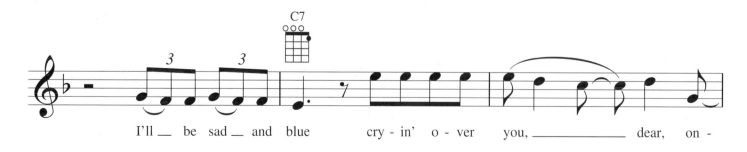

I'll ___ be sad ___ and blue cry-in' o-ver you, ___ dear, on-

Love Me Tender

Words and Music by Elvis Presley and Vera Matson

First note

Moderately slow

1. Love me _____ ten - der, love me sweet. ___

Nev - er let me go. ___ You have made ___ my life ___

_____ com - plete, ___ and ___ I ___ love you so. _____

Love me ten - der, love ___ me true. ___ All _____ my dreams ful-

fill. For my dar - lin', ___

and I al - ways will. _____   3. Love me ten - der,

love me dear. _   Tell _____ me _ you are _____ mine.

I'll be yours _ through all _____ the years; _____ till the end of

time.   Love me ten - der,   love _ me true. _   All _

_____ my dreams _ ful - fill.   For my dar - ling, _____

I _____ love you, _   and _____ I al - ways _ will.

Loving You

Words and Music by Jerry Leiber and Mike Stoller

First note

Moderately slow

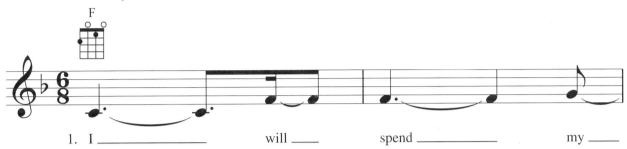

1. I _____ will _____ spend _____ my _____

_____ whole life _____ through _____ lov - ing

you, _____ just _____ lov - ing you. _____

Win - ter, sum - mer, _____ spring - time too, _____

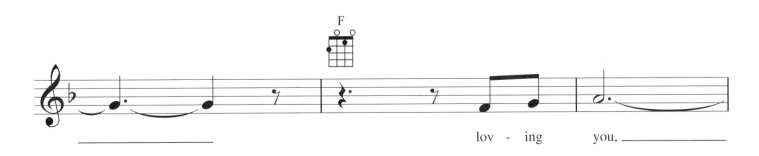

_____ lov - ing you, _____

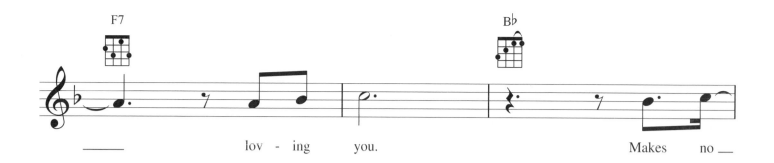

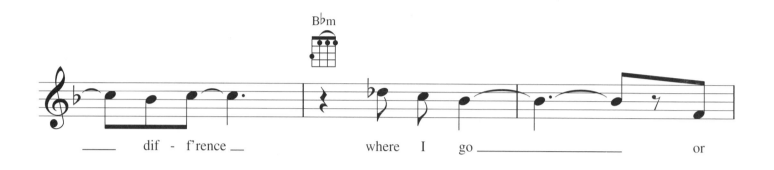

_____ lov - ing you. Makes no _____

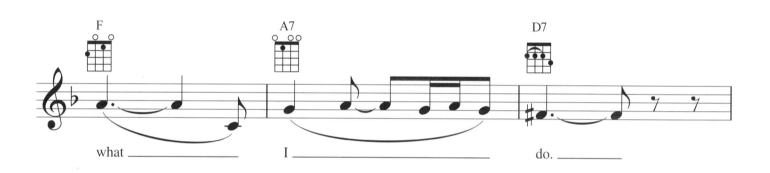

_____ dif - f'rence _____ where I go _____ or

what _____ I _____ do. _____

You know that _____ I'll _____

_____ al - ways be _____ lov -

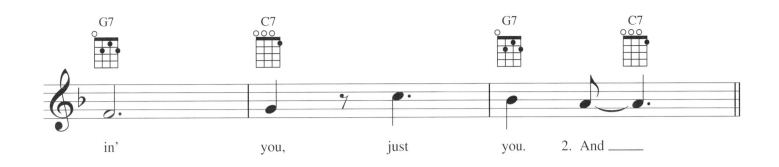

in'   you,   just   you.   2. And _____

if   I'm   seen _____ with _____ some - one   new, _____

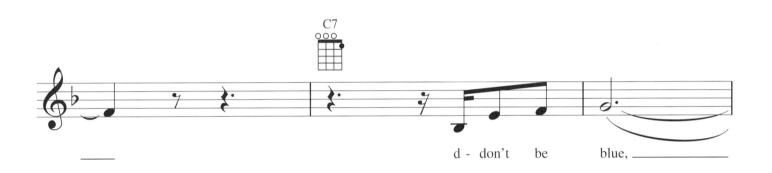

_____   d - don't   be   blue, _____

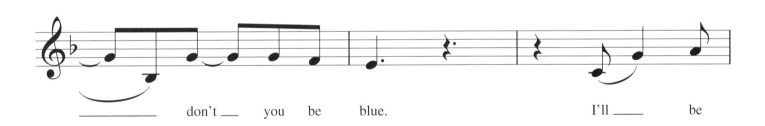

_____ don't __ you   be   blue.   I'll __ be

faith - ful, _____   I'll __ be   true, _____

Return to Sender

Words and Music by Otis Blackwell and Winfield Scott

First note

Moderately

Re - turn ___ to send - er.

Re - turn ___ to send - er.   1. I gave a let - ter to the

post - man, ___   he put it in his sack. ___

Bright and ear - ly next morn - in', ___   he brought my let - ter

back.   Re - turn ___ to send - er,

ad - dress un - known.   No such

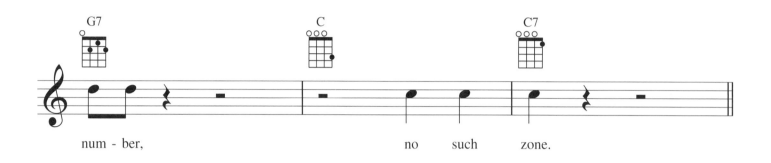

num - ber,   no such zone.

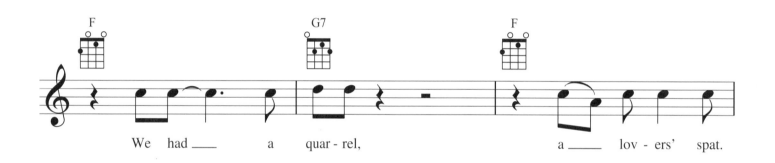

We had ___ a quar - rel,   a ___ lov - ers' spat.

I ___ write, "I'm sor - ry," but my

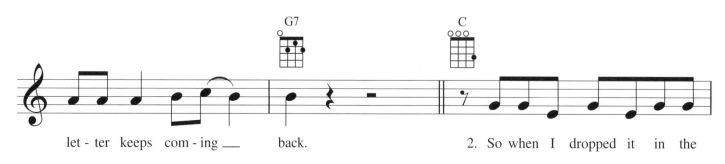

let - ter keeps com - ing ___ back.   2. So when I dropped it in the

mail - box, ___ and sent it spe - cial D.,

bright and ear - ly next morn - in', ___ it came right back to ___

me. Re - turn ___ to send - er,

ad - dress un - known. No such

per - son, no such zone.

This time, ___ I'm gon - na take it my - self and put it right in ___ her hand. ___

_____ And if it comes back the ver - y next day,

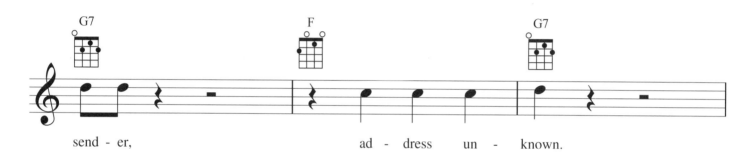

then I'll un - der - stand. _____ Re - turn _____ to

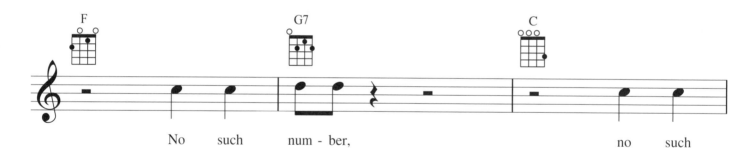

send - er, ad - dress un - known.

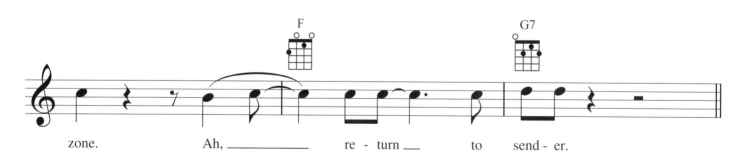

No such num - ber, no such

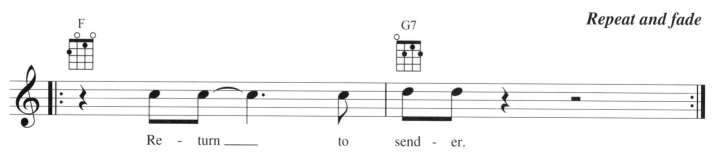

zone. Ah, _____ re - turn _____ to send - er.

Repeat and fade

Re - turn _____ to send - er.

Suspicious Minds

Words and Music by Francis Zambon

First note
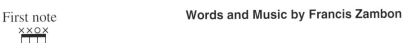

Moderately fast

1. We're caught in a trap. _____
2. So if an old friend I know _____

I can't walk out, _____
stops by to say hel - lo, _____

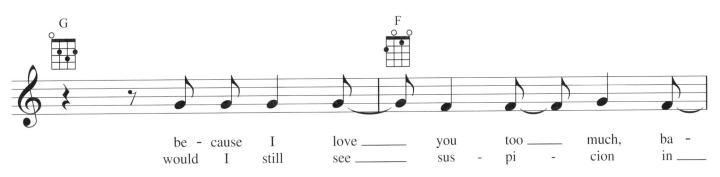

be - cause I love _____ you too _____ much, ba -
would I still see _____ sus - pi - cion in _____

- by. _____
your _____ eyes? _____

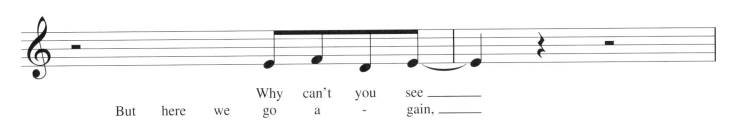

Why can't you see _____
But here we go a - gain, _____

what you're do - ing to me _____
ask - ing where I've _____ been. _____

when you don't be - lieve _____ a word ___ I say? __
You can't see the tears _____ are real _____ I'm cry -

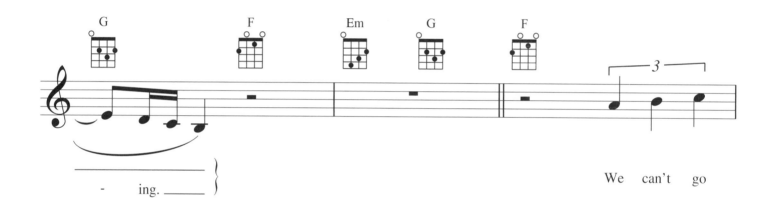

- ing. _____

We can't go

on to - geth - er with sus - pi - cious minds, __

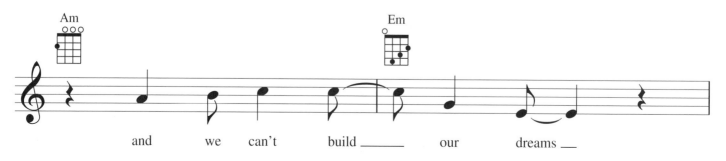

and we can't build _____ our dreams __

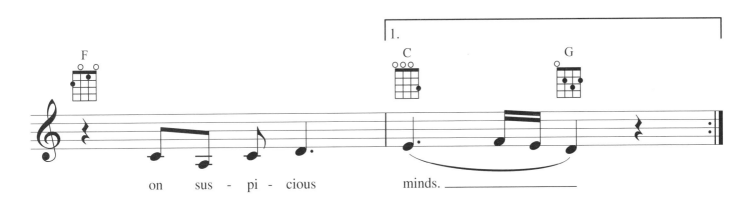

on sus - pi - cious minds. _____

minds. _____ Oh, let our love sur - vive, _____

or drive the tears from your eyes. _____ Let's don't let a

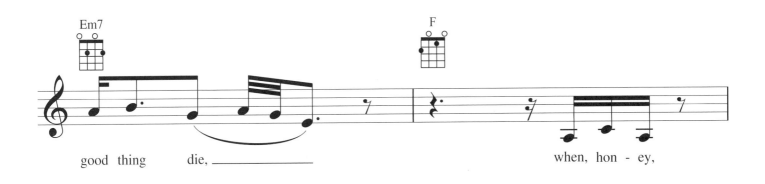

good thing die, _____ when, hon - ey,

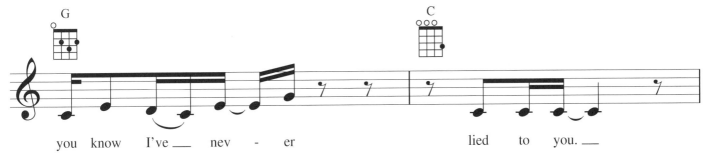

you know I've _ nev - er lied to you. _

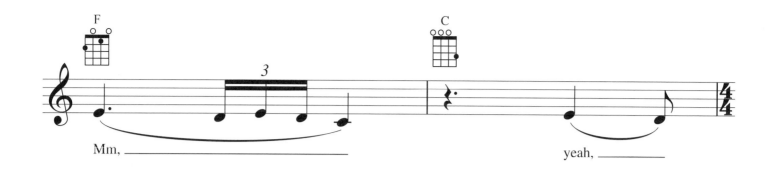

Mm, _____

yeah, _____

yeah. ___

3. We're caught in a trap. ___

I can't walk out, ____

be - cause ___ I love ___

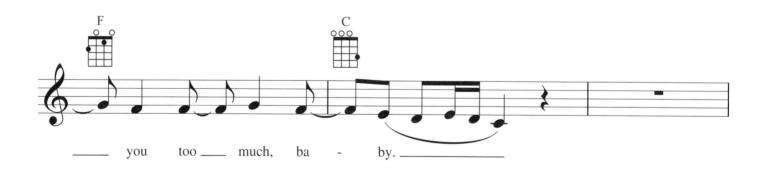

_____ you too ___ much, ba - by. _____

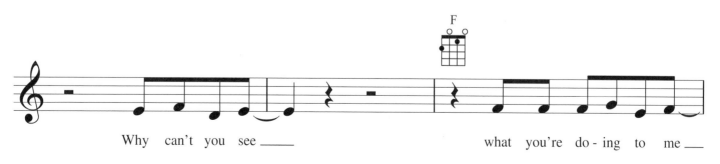

Why can't you see _____

what you're do - ing to me ___

62

Repeat and fade

(Let Me Be Your) Teddy Bear

First note

Words and Music by Kal Mann and Bernie Lowe

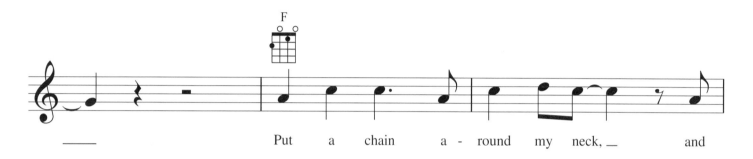

1. A ba - by, let me be _____ your lov - in' ted - dy bear. _____

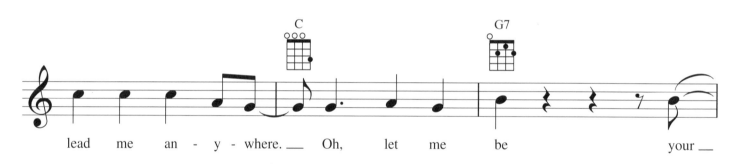

_____ Put a chain a - round my neck, _____ and

lead me an - y - where. _____ Oh, let me be your _____

_____ ted - dy bear. I

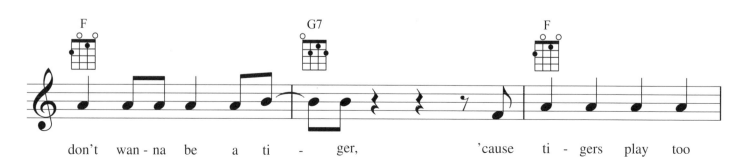

don't wan - na be a ti - ger, 'cause ti - gers play too

rough.   I   don't wan - na be a li - on,   'cause

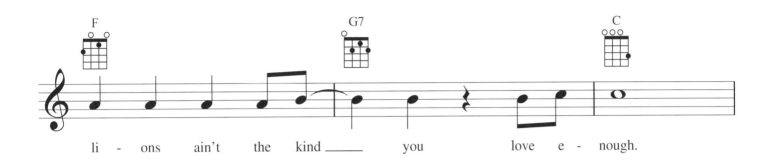

li - ons ain't the kind _____ you   love e - nough.

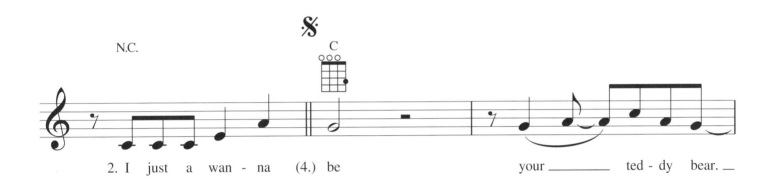

2. I just a wan - na (4.) be   your _____ ted - dy bear. _

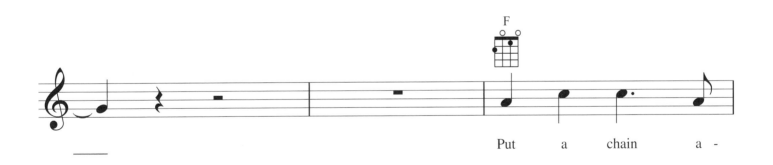

_____   Put a chain a -

To Coda

round my neck, __   and lead me an - y - where. __ Oh, let me

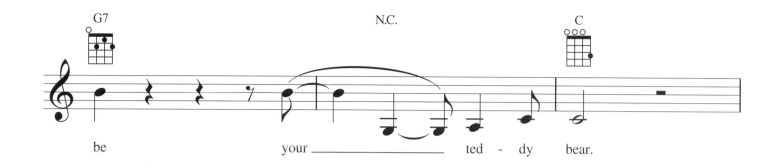

be   your   ted - dy   bear.

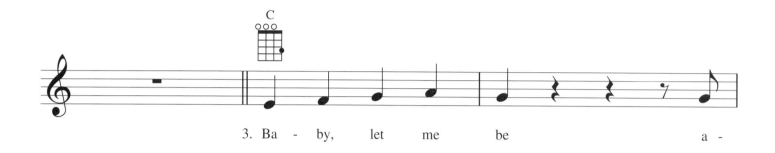

3. Ba - by,   let   me   be   a -

round   you   ev - 'ry   night. ___   Run   your   fin - gers

through my hair ___   and   cud - dle   me   real   tight.   Oh,   let   me

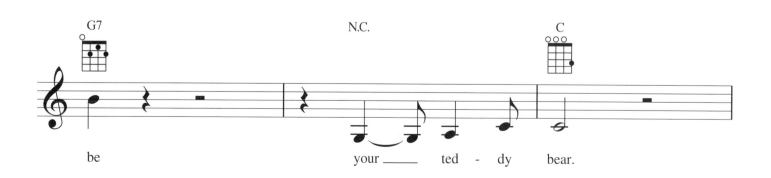

be   your ___   ted - dy   bear.

Too Much

Words and Music by Lee Rosenberg and Bernard Weinman

First note

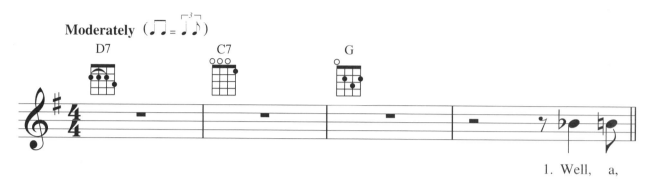

1. Well, a,

hon - ey, I ___ love you too much. I need ___ your ___ lov - in'

too much. Want ___ the thrill of your touch. ___ Well, a,

gee, I can't love ___ you too much. You do all the liv - in' while I ___

___ do all the giv - in' 'cause I love you too much. 2. Well,

you spend all my mon - ey   too much.   I   have to share you, hon - ey,

too much.   When ___ I want some lov - in',   you're gone. ___   A,

don't you know you're treat - in'   your dad - dy wrong? _   Now you got me start - ed, don't you

leave me brok - en heart - ed 'cause I   love   you   too   much.   3. I ___

need _ your _ lov - in'   all   the   time. ___   Need   your   hug - gin',

please   be   mine. _   Need   you   near   me,   stay   real   close. _   Oh,

please, please, hear me, you're the most. _ Now you got me start - ed, don't you

leave me bro - ken heart - ed 'cause I love you too much. 4. Well, ev -

- 'ry time I kiss, a, your _ sweet lips, I _____ can feel my heart, a, go _____

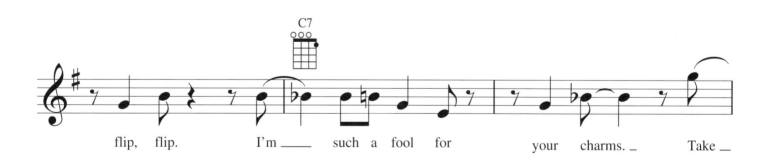

flip, flip. I'm _____ such a fool for your charms. _ Take _

_____ me back, a, ba - by, in your arms. _ Like to hear you sigh - in' e - ven

though I know you're ly - in' 'cause I love you too much. 5. I _____

need _ your _ lov - in' all the time. _ I need _ your _ hug - gin',

please be mine. _ I need a, you _ near me, stay real close.

Please, please, a, hear me, you're the most. _ Now you got me start - ed, don't you

leave me brok - en heart - ed 'cause I love you too much.

Jim Beloff

Jim Beloff is the author of *The Ukulele—A Visual History* (Backbeat Books) and author, arranger, and publisher of the popular Jumpin' Jim's series of ukulele songbooks. This series is sold worldwide and is distributed by the Hal Leonard Corporation.

Jim has also recorded two CDs of original songs performed on the ukulele (*Jim's Dog Has Fleas* and *For the Love of Uke*), produced *Legends of Ukulele*, a CD compilation for Rhino Records, and made two how-to-play DVDs for Homespun Tapes, *The Joy of Uke #1* and *#2*. In November 1999, he premiered his *Uke Can't Be Serious* concerto for ukulele and symphony orchestra. It was commissioned and performed with the Wallingford (Connecticut) Symphony. In 2004, he released *The Finer Things*, a recording of sixteen songs he co-wrote with ukulele master Herb Ohta.

In 1999, Jim and his family introduced a new, colorful, and low-cost ukulele called the Fluke and later a soprano-sized model, the Flea, that have won admirers all over the world. Jim and his wife Liz own Flea Market Music, Inc., a company dedicated to the ukulele. They believe very strongly in their company's motto, "Uke Can Change the World." You can reach Jim through the Flea Market Music web site at **www.fleamarketmusic.com**.

Photo by Elizabeth Maihock Beloff

Jim Beloff at the Graceland gate in Memphis, Tennessee.